LITTLE LIBRARY

Jet Airliners

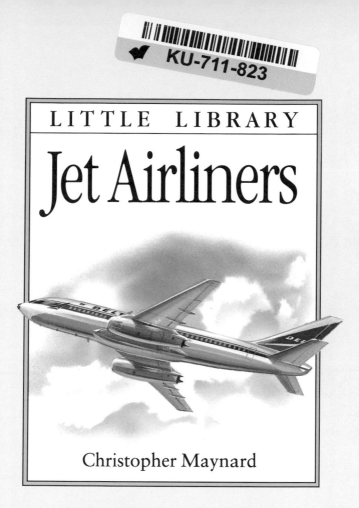

Christopher Maynard

Kingfisher Books

Contents

Air travel

More than 500 million people travel by air every year, and the number is growing.

Today, you can board a jet plane any morning of the week, fly around the world and arrive back home within two to three days. However, just over 100 years ago, before aircraft had been invented, to go around the world even in 80 days was thought of as an astonishing adventure.

Inside the plane

A part from Concorde, all airliners have the same basic shape and have similar features to the Airbus A320 below. The passengers sit in the long tube-shaped cabin, and the pilot flies the plane from the flight deck at the front.

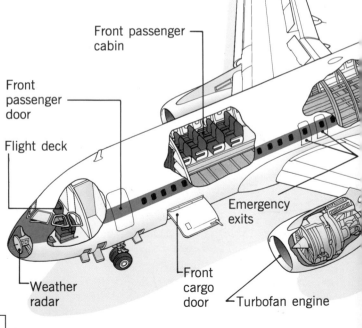

Front passenger cabin

Front passenger door

Flight deck

Emergency exits

Weather radar

Front cargo door

Turbofan engine

The Airbus A320 is a type of jet that is often used on medium-length routes, for example from London to Madrid in Spain. It flies at about 800 km/h and can carry up to 180 passengers.

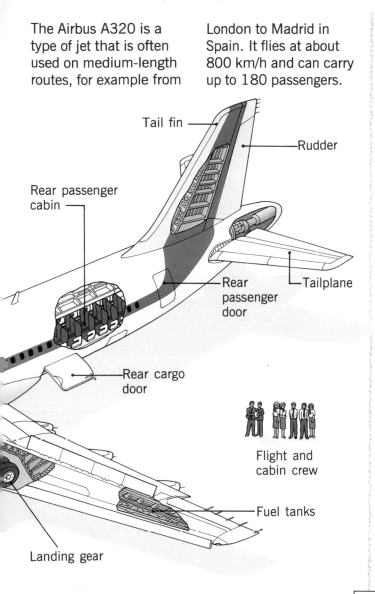

Tail fin

Rudder

Rear passenger cabin

Rear passenger door

Tailplane

Rear cargo door

Flight and cabin crew

Fuel tanks

Landing gear

How planes fly

How does a fully-loaded Jumbo jet weighing over 300 tonnes stay in the air? The secret is in the wings.

The jet's wings have a rounded shape called an aerofoil. When fast-flowing air passes over them it pulls them up. This pull is called lift. When the lift is greater than the plane's weight, it flies.

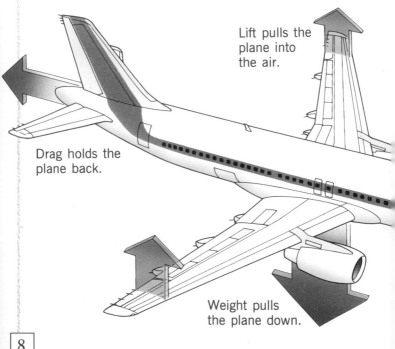

Lift pulls the plane into the air.

Drag holds the plane back.

Weight pulls the plane down.

You can try this experiment to see how the wings of a plane lift in moving air.

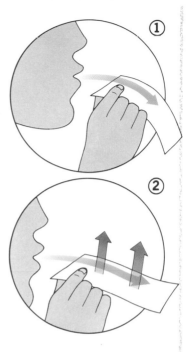

1 Hold one end of a sheet of paper up to your lips. Let the other end flop. Blow hard across the top.

2 The paper lifts because air is moving fast over the top of it. This lowers the pressure or weight of air above the paper. Because the air pressure underneath is greater, it lifts the paper up.

There are four forces at work on a plane in flight. **Lift** from the wings keeps it in the air. The amount of lift has to be more than the **weight** of the plane, which pulls it down. The **drag** of the air holds the plane back, so the jet's engines must produce enough **thrust** to push it forwards.

Thrust pushes the plane fowards.

Steering

A ll planes have moving parts on the wings which the pilot uses to help steer the plane. Elevators on the tailplane are for diving or climbing. Ailerons on the wings work in pairs, and make a plane roll, or bank into a turn. The rudder on the tail steadies the plane so it doesn't swing to and fro.

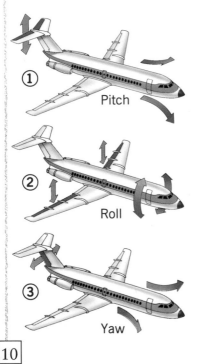

① Pitch

② Roll

③ Yaw

1 Elevators change the pitch, or angle of the plane. Lowering them points the nose down, making the plane dive. Raising them points the nose up, making the plane climb.

2 Ailerons make the plane roll, or bank. For example, if the left aileron is up, that side of the plane will dip.

3 The rudder controls the side-to-side movement of the plane, known as yawing.

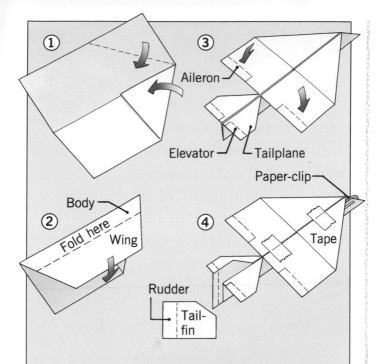

① ② Body — Fold here Wing ③ Aileron — Elevator — Tailplane Paper-clip — Tape ④ Rudder — Tail-fin

MAKE A GLIDER

1 Fold a square of stiff paper in half. Turn in two corners.
2 Close the two sides. Fold back each side to make a wing. Leave a body about 3 cm deep.
3 Cut into the wings to make a tailplane. Cut and fold elevators and wing ailerons.
4 Weight the nose with a paper-clip. Tape the wings so they don't open in flight.

Cut out a tailfin and make a fold in it for the rudder. Glue the tailfin into the back of the glider.

11

Engines

Today, most airliners are fitted with jet engines. Some planes have two, while others have three or four. The engines may be mounted on the wings, the main body, or on the tail.

A JET BALLOON

Blow up a balloon and pinch the neck. Then let go of it. The air rushes out with so much force that it sends the balloon flying across the room.

Balloon shoots forwards

Air shoots backwards

Engines on the wings

Engines at the rear

Engines on the wings and tail

INSIDE A TURBOFAN JET

1 At the front of this jet, a fan sucks in air. Some goes around the engine, some into it.

2 In the compressor, the air is squeezed to pack as much as possible into the combustion chamber.

3 Fuel is sprayed into the combustion chamber and is set alight. It burns to make hot gases.

4 The hot gases roar through the turbine making it spin round very fast. The turbine drives the compressor and the fan.

5 Escaping hot gases, and the cold air from the fan, create the thrust that drives the plane forwards.

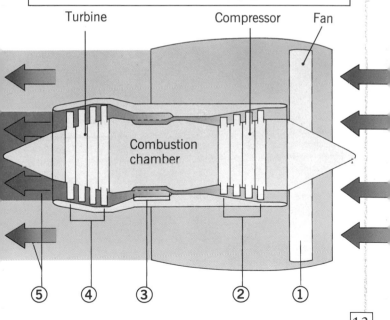

Turbine   Compressor   Fan

Combustion chamber

⑤   ④   ③   ②   ①

The flight deck

M ost jets are flown by two people, the pilot and the copilot. The pilot steers the plane with the U-shaped control column, or stick, while the co-pilot checks the instruments to make sure everything is working as it should be and the plane is on course.

FLIGHT INSTRUMENTS

1 The airspeed indicator shows the plane's speed.

2 The altimeter shows how high the plane is flying.

3 The artificial horizon shows if the plane is flying level to the ground.

① Airspeed indicator

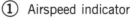

② Altimeter

③ Artificial horizon

Check-in

E very plane journey starts at an airport. Whether passengers are travelling on business or going on holiday, the first thing everyone does is go to the check-in desk of the airline they are flying with. There, tickets are checked, and luggage is weighed and labelled with the flight number.

AT THE AIRPORT

After checking-in your luggage you will be given a boarding pass. Without this you will not be able to board the plane.

On your way to the departure lounge, you will first be asked to show your passport and then go through a security check.

1 Check the time of your flight and the gate at which you board the plane.

2 As you go through passport control, you will need to show your passport.

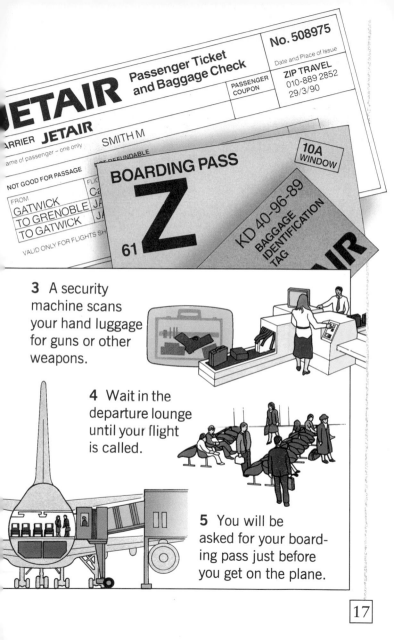

No. 508975

JETAIR
Passenger Ticket
and Baggage Check

PASSENGER COUPON

Date and Place of Issue

ZIP TRAVEL
010-889 2852
29/3/90

CARRIER **JETAIR**

SMITH M

Name of passenger – one only

NOT REFUNDABLE

NOT GOOD FOR PASSAGE

FROM
GATWICK
TO GRENOBLE
TO GATWICK

VALID ONLY FOR FLIGHTS SH

BOARDING PASS

Z

61

10A
WINDOW

KD 40-96-89
BAGGAGE
IDENTIFICATION
TAG

3 A security machine scans your hand luggage for guns or other weapons.

4 Wait in the departure lounge until your flight is called.

5 You will be asked for your boarding pass just before you get on the plane.

Ground crew

T housands of people work behind the scenes at busy airports. Their job is to make sure everything runs smoothly, safely, and on time.

△ Airport firetrucks are fitted with powerful spray guns that smother fires with thick foam.

▽ In snowy weather, the main runways are cleared so planes can land safely.

△ Hose trucks connect planes to fuel tanks under the ground.

GROUND SIGNALS

When a plane arrives at the airport terminal a marshal is waiting to direct the pilot into a parking bay.

Jet engines make a lot of noise, so the marshals wear ear muffs and use bats to signal instructions to the pilot.

Practise these signals yourself with a set of ping-pong bats. You could try guiding a friend on a bike into a 'parking bay' near your home.

Move forward   Over here   Turn left

Turn right   Stop   Stop engines

The next flight

At a very busy airport, planes land or take off every few minutes all day and sometimes at night as well.

Planes don't make money sitting on the ground, so as soon as the plane stops outside the terminal, the ground crew gets busy preparing the plane for the next flight.

Luggage is unloaded on to baggage trucks. Food for the next flight arrives on the catering trucks, while cleaners prepare the passenger cabin.

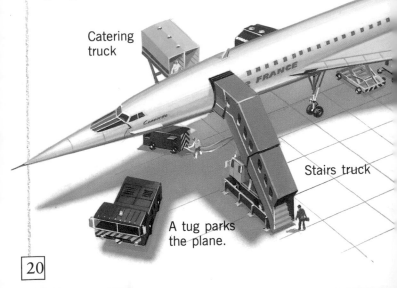

Catering truck

Stairs truck

A tug parks the plane.

Concorde cruises at 2300 km/h and can fly its 128 passengers across the Atlantic in 3 hours. Between flights its tanks are filled with fuel and its kitchens with fresh food.

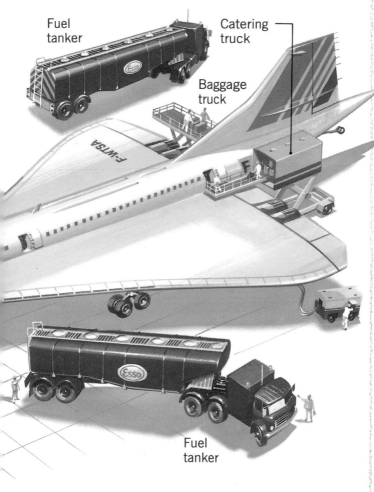

Fuel tanker

Catering truck

Baggage truck

Fuel tanker

Air traffic control

T he duty of air traffic control is to direct planes safely through the space they control, both in the air and on the ground. Through the windows of their tower, the controllers watch planes on the runway and in the skies near the airport. They also have lots of radar screens to track planes that are out of sight.

④

②

①

③

TAKING OFF

1 Air traffic control gives the pilot permission to move.

2 The pilot moves the plane from the parking bay.

3 The pilot slowly taxis the plane to the waiting area near the runway.

4 Air traffic control gives permission to take-off. The pilot moves the plane on to the main runway, builds up to full speed and engine power and takes off.

RADIO ALPHABET

Air traffic controllers talk to pilots by radio when they give them permission to take off and land, or tell them which route to fly.

Over the radio, the plane is always identified with its registration name, and words are used for the letters which make up the name. Then nobody can mistake which plane the controllers mean.

If the registration number of your plane is G-GRWL, how would you identify it?

A	Alpha	N	November
B	Bravo	O	Oscar
C	Charlie	P	Papa
D	Delta	Q	Quebec
E	Echo	R	Romeo
F	Foxtrot	S	Sierra
G	Golf	T	Tango
H	Hotel	U	Uniform
I	India	V	Victor
J	Juliet	W	Whisky
K	Kilo	X	X-ray
L	Lima	Y	Yankee
M	Mike	Z	Zulu

Take-off

As soon as the plane has been refuelled, the baggage is loaded and the passengers come on board. The cabin doors are shut and the pilot taxis the plane to the main runway. Once air traffic control gives the go-ahead, the engines build up to full power, the brakes are released and the plane races down the runway and takes off.

Really big jets need a long runway so they can build up enough speed to take off. Some runways can be as long as 5 km which gives a Jumbo plenty of room to take off safely.

When flight speed is reached, the nose wheel lifts first, then the main wheels follow. At the point where a Jumbo's wheels leave the ground it is travelling at about 278 km/h.

Over 55 years

The first regular passenger flights began in 1914. Since then, the size of airliners has grown enormously. Today, one of the biggest airliners of all, the Boeing 747–400, can carry more than 400 passengers at a time.

1969: Boeing 747.
First jumbo jet

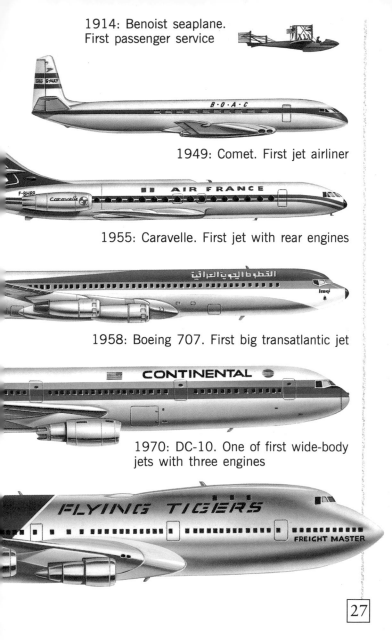

1914: Benoist seaplane.
First passenger service

1949: Comet. First jet airliner

1955: Caravelle. First jet with rear engines

1958: Boeing 707. First big transatlantic jet

1970: DC-10. One of first wide-body
jets with three engines

27

Plane spotting

A irlines use so many different kinds of planes it takes some practice to tell them apart. Look out for these the next time you visit an airport.

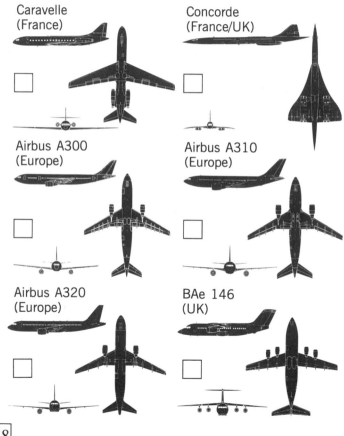

Caravelle
(France)

Concorde
(France/UK)

Airbus A300
(Europe)

Airbus A310
(Europe)

Airbus A320
(Europe)

BAe 146
(UK)

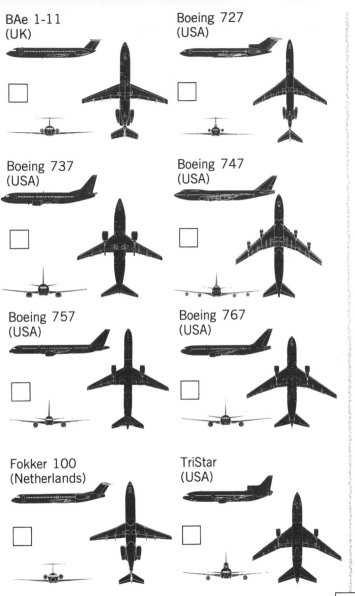

BAe 1-11
(UK)

Boeing 727
(USA)

Boeing 737
(USA)

Boeing 747
(USA)

Boeing 757
(USA)

Boeing 767
(USA)

Fokker 100
(Netherlands)

TriStar
(USA)

Index